Hal•Leonard
JAZZ PLAY-ALONG®

Book and CD for B♭, E♭, C and Bass Clef Instruments

VOLUME 92

Leonard Bernstein®
10 FAVORITE SONGS

Arranged and Produced by Mark Taylor and Jim Roberts

BOOK

CD

ISBN 978-1-4234-5822-7

LEONARD BERNSTEIN
Music Publishing
Company LLC

Boosey & Hawkes

Hal•Leonard®
CORPORATION

7777 W. BLUEMOUND RD. P.O. BOX 13819 MILWAUKEE, WI 53213

Visit Hal Leonard Online at
www.halleonard.com

LEONARD BERNSTEIN

Volume 92

Arranged and Produced by
Mark Taylor and Jim Roberts

Featured Players:

Graham Breedlove–Trumpet
John Desalme–Saxes
Tony Nalker–Piano
Jim Roberts–Bass
Joe McCarthy–Drums

**Recorded at Bias Studios, Springfield, Virginia
Bob Dawson, Engineer**

HOW TO USE THE CD:

Each song has <u>two</u> tracks:

1) Split Track/Melody

Woodwind, Brass, Keyboard, and **Mallet Players** can use this track as a learning tool for melody style and inflection.

Bass Players can learn and perform with this track – remove the recorded bass track by turning down the volume on the LEFT channel.

Keyboard and **Guitar Players** can learn and perform with this track – remove the recorded piano part by turning down the volume on the RIGHT channel.

2) Full Stereo Track

Soloists or **Groups** can learn and perform with this accompaniment track with the RHYTHM SECTION only.

CD

1: SPLIT TRACK/MELODY
2: FULL STEREO TRACK

C VERSION

COOL
FROM WEST SIDE STORY ®

LYRICS BY STEPHEN SONDHEIM
MUSIC BY LEONARD BERNSTEIN ®

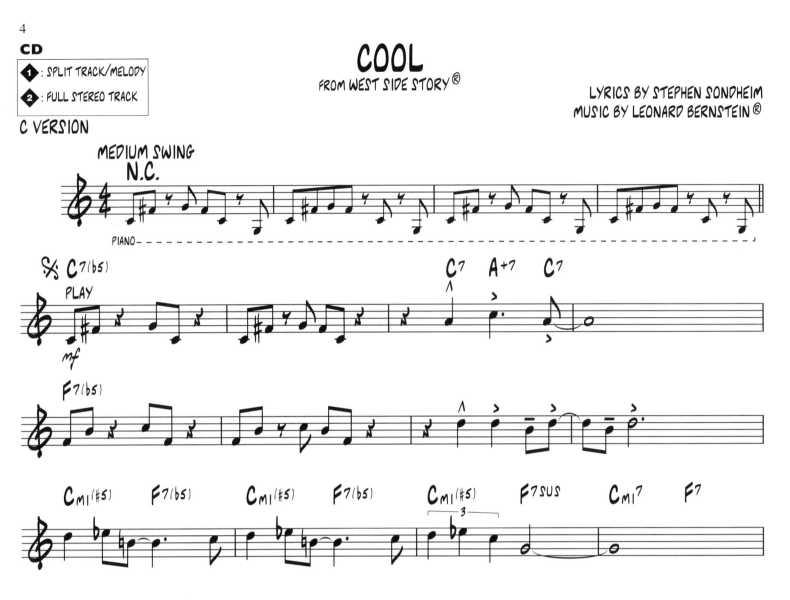

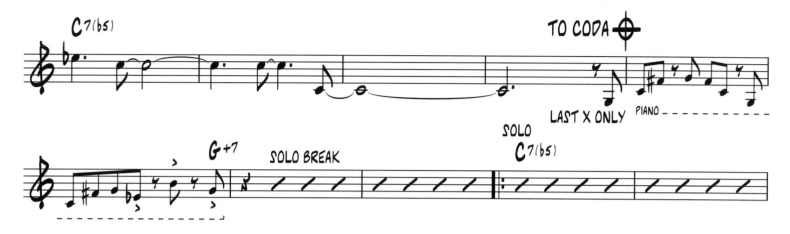

CD
- ③ : SPLIT TRACK/MELODY
- ④ : FULL STEREO TRACK

C VERSION

I FEEL PRETTY
FROM WEST SIDE STORY ®

LYRICS BY STEPHEN SONDHEIM
MUSIC BY LEONARD BERNSTEIN ®

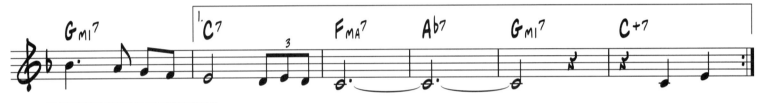

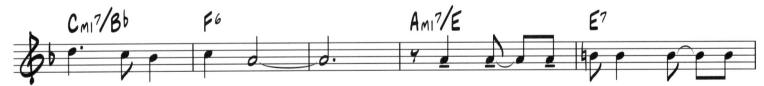

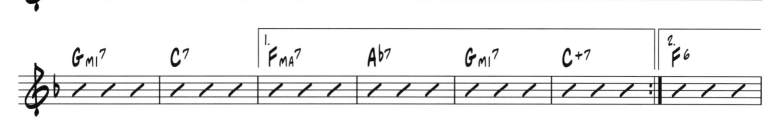

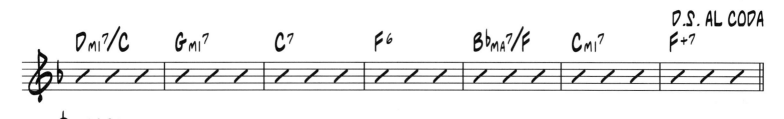

JET SONG

FROM WEST SIDE STORY®

LYRICS BY STEPHEN SONDHEIM
MUSIC BY LEONARD BERNSTEIN®

CD

5: SPLIT TRACK/MELODY
6: FULL STEREO TRACK

C VERSION

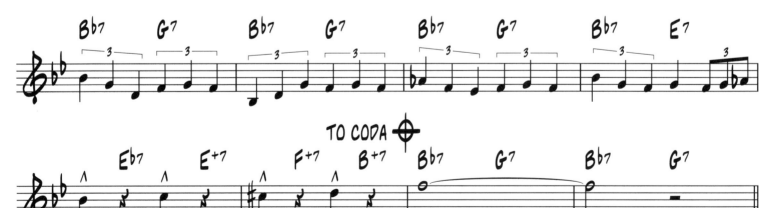

SOLOS (2 CHORUSES)

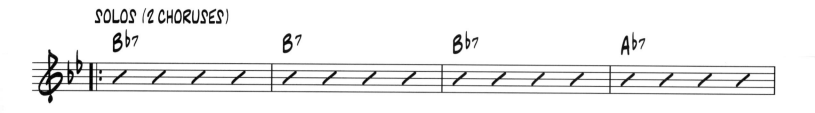

D.S. AL CODA

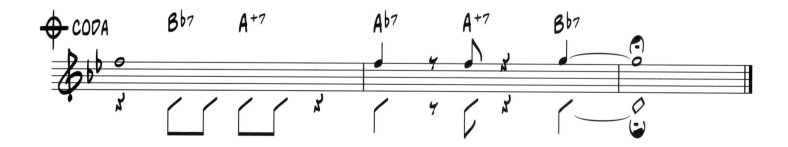

LUCKY TO BE ME
FROM ON THE TOWN

WORDS BY BETTY COMDEN AND ADOLPH GREEN
MUSIC BY LEONARD BERNSTEIN ®

C VERSION

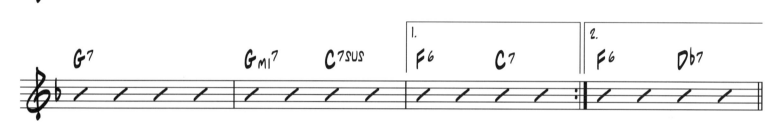

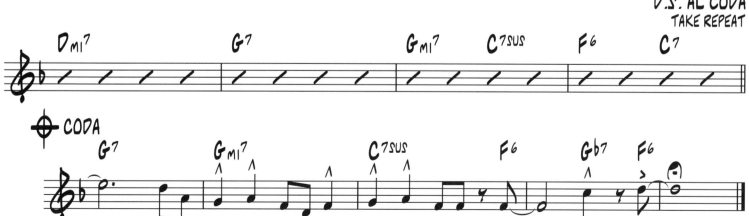

CD
9 : SPLIT TRACK/MELODY
10 : FULL STEREO TRACK

MAMBO FROM THE DANCE AT THE GYM
FROM WEST SIDE STORY®

LYRICS BY STEPHEN SONDHEIM
MUSIC BY LEONARD BERNSTEIN®

C VERSION

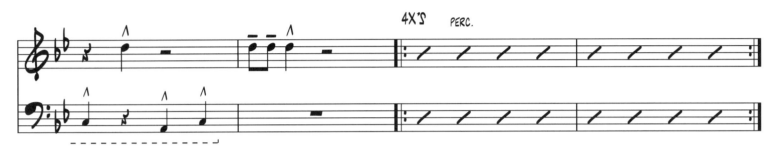

CD

🔷 11 : SPLIT TRACK/MELODY
🔷 12 : FULL STEREO TRACK

C VERSION

MARIA
FROM WEST SIDE STORY ®

LYRICS BY STEPHEN SONDHEIM
MUSIC BY LEONARD BERNSTEIN ®

SOLO
C6 | | | | GmA7/B | C6 GmA7

Dmi7 G7sus | CmA7 | C6 | |

G6/B | Ami7 Emi7 | Ami7 Emi7 | Bmi7 /F#

F6 | | Emi7 | Gmi7

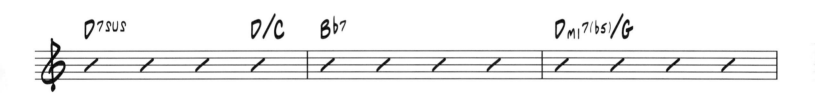

D7sus | D/C Bb7 | | Dmi7(b5)/G

C6 | Db6 | C6 | Db6 D.S. AL CODA

CODA
FmA7 | | Eb6 | 3 | 3

Db6 | | Bb7 | CmA7

CD

15 : SPLIT TRACK/MELODY
16 : FULL STEREO TRACK

C VERSION

SOME OTHER TIME
FROM ON THE TOWN

WORDS BY BETTY COMDEN AND ADOLPH GREEN
MUSIC BY LEONARD BERNSTEIN®

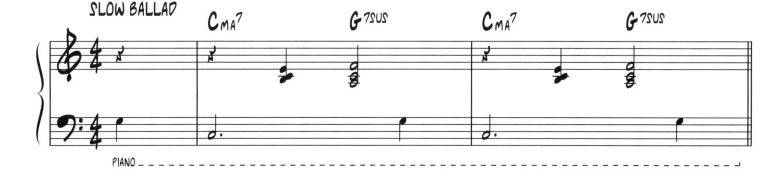

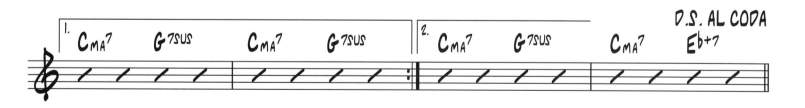

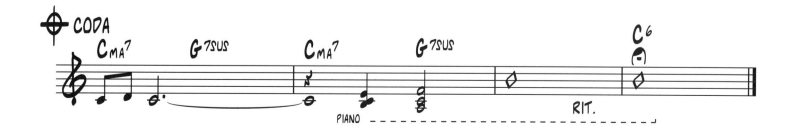

Somewhere
FROM WEST SIDE STORY®

LYRICS BY STEPHEN SONDHEIM
MUSIC BY LEONARD BERNSTEIN®

C VERSION

SLOW BALLAD

TONIGHT
FROM WEST SIDE STORY ®

LYRICS BY STEPHEN SONDHEIM
MUSIC BY LEONARD BERNSTEIN ®

CD
⟨19⟩ : SPLIT TRACK/MELODY
⟨20⟩ : FULL STEREO TRACK

C VERSION

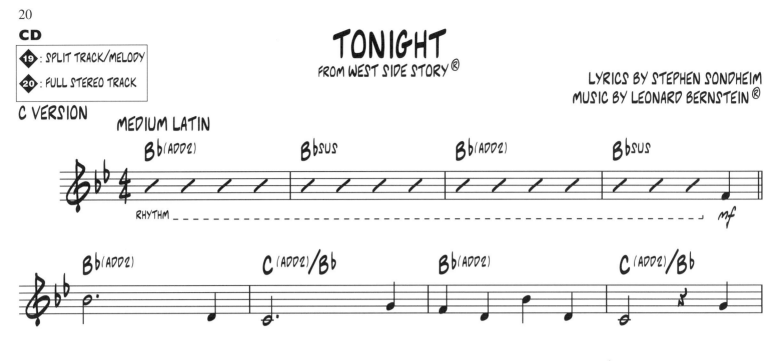

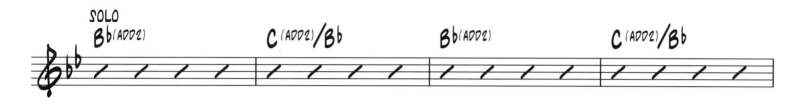

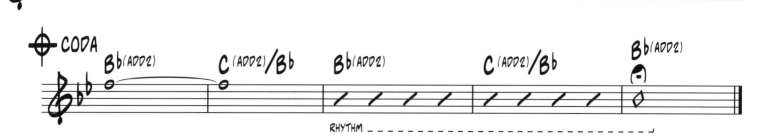

CD

13 : SPLIT TRACK/MELODY
14 : FULL STEREO TRACK

C VERSION

NEW YORK, NEW YORK

FROM ON THE TOWN ®

WORDS BY BETTY COMDEN AND ADOLPH GREEN
MUSIC BY LEONARD BERNSTEIN ®

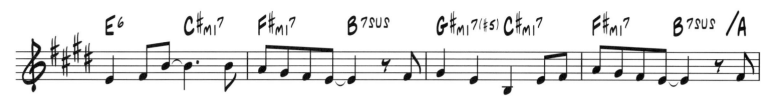

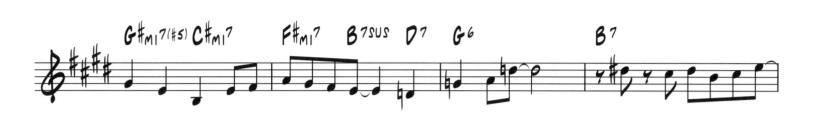

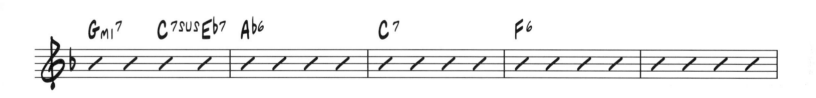

NEW YORK, NEW YORK

FROM ON THE TOWN ®

WORDS BY BETTY COMDEN AND ADOLPH GREEN
MUSIC BY LEONARD BERNSTEIN ®

Bb VERSION

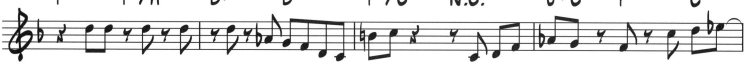

26

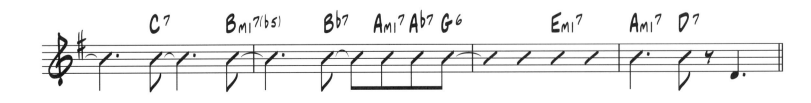

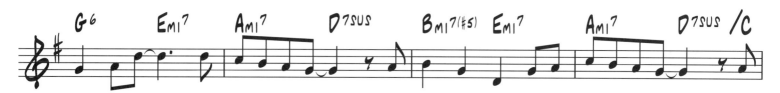

CD
❶ : SPLIT TRACK/MELODY
❷ : FULL STEREO TRACK

COOL
FROM WEST SIDE STORY ®

LYRICS BY STEPHEN SONDHEIM
MUSIC BY LEONARD BERNSTEIN ®

Bb VERSION

MEDIUM SWING

PIANO

I FEEL PRETTY
FROM WEST SIDE STORY®

LYRICS BY STEPHEN SONDHEIM
MUSIC BY LEONARD BERNSTEIN®

Bb VERSION

MEDIUM JAZZ WALTZ

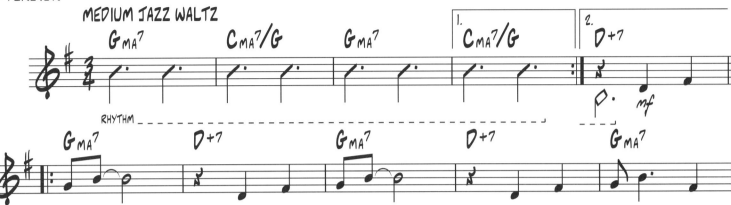

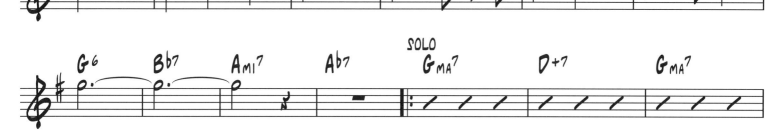

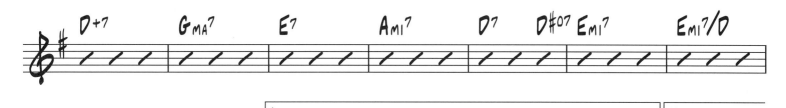

CD
5 : SPLIT TRACK/MELODY
6 : FULL STEREO TRACK

Bb VERSION

JET SONG
FROM WEST SIDE STORY ®

LYRICS BY STEPHEN SONDHEIM
MUSIC BY LEONARD BERNSTEIN ®

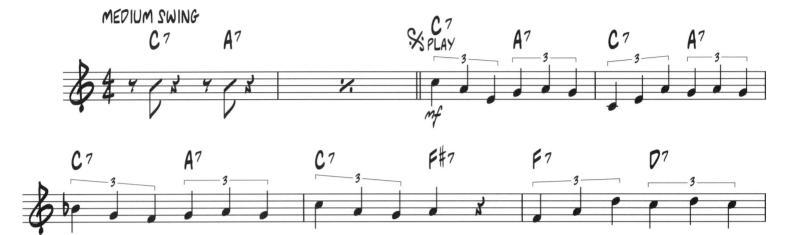

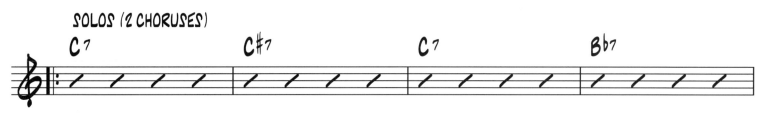

SOLOS (2 CHORUSES)

C7 · C#7 · C7 · Bb7

C7 · C#7 · C7 · F#7

F7 · F#7 · F7 · Eb7

C7 · C#7 · C7 · Bb7

A7

D.S. AL CODA

D7 · G7

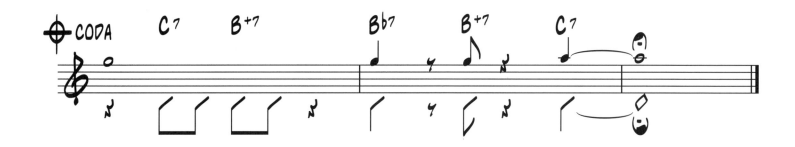

CODA · C7 · B+7 · Bb7 · B+7 · C7

LUCKY TO BE ME

FROM ON THE TOWN

WORDS BY BETTY COMDEN AND ADOLPH GREEN
MUSIC BY LEONARD BERNSTEIN ®

CD

◆7 : SPLIT TRACK/MELODY
◆8 : FULL STEREO TRACK

Bb VERSION

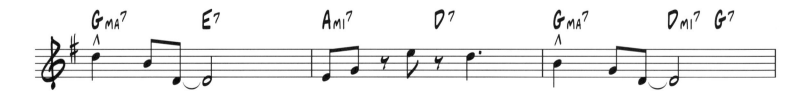

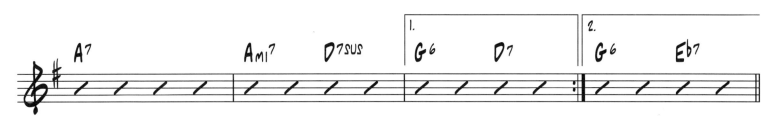

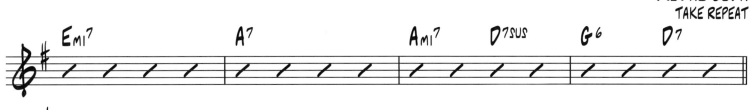

Mambo from The Dance at the Gym

FROM WEST SIDE STORY®

LYRICS BY STEPHEN SONDHEIM
MUSIC BY LEONARD BERNSTEIN ®

Bb VERSION

CD

⓫ : SPLIT TRACK/MELODY

⓬ : FULL STEREO TRACK

MARIA
FROM WEST SIDE STORY®

LYRICS BY STEPHEN SONDHEIM
MUSIC BY LEONARD BERNSTEIN®

Bb VERSION

SLOW LATIN

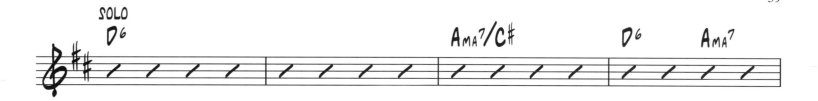

SOLO

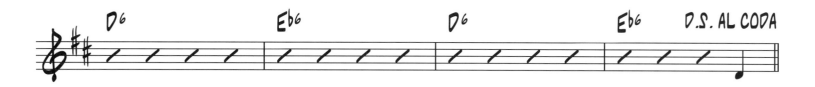

CODA

SOME OTHER TIME

FROM ON THE TOWN

WORDS BY BETTY COMDEN AND ADOLPH GREEN
MUSIC BY LEONARD BERNSTEIN ®

Bb VERSION

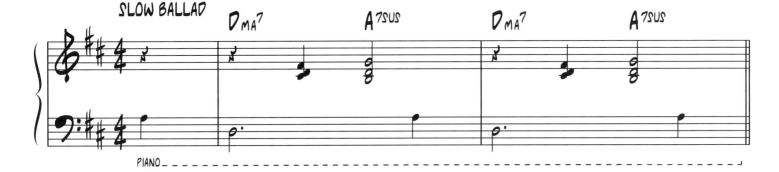

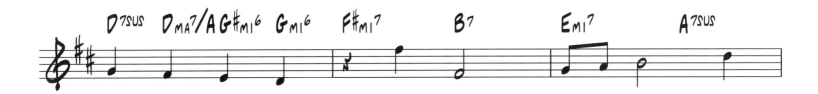

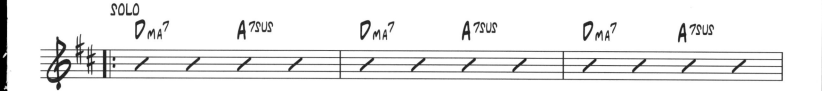

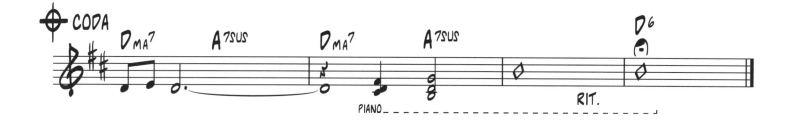

Somewhere
FROM WEST SIDE STORY ®

LYRICS BY STEPHEN SONDHEIM
MUSIC BY LEONARD BERNSTEIN ®

Bb VERSION

SLOW BALLAD

43

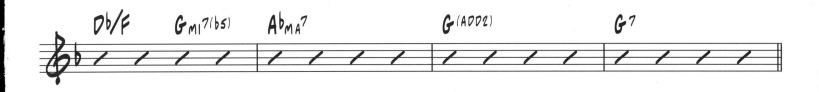

CD

- **19**: SPLIT TRACK/MELODY
- **20**: FULL STEREO TRACK

TONIGHT
FROM WEST SIDE STORY ®

LYRICS BY STEPHEN SONDHEIM
MUSIC BY LEONARD BERNSTEIN ®

Bb VERSION

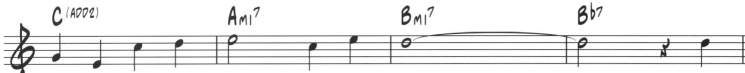

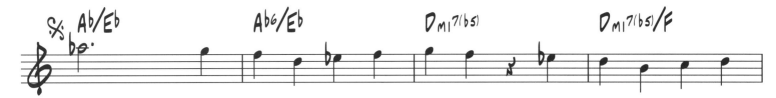

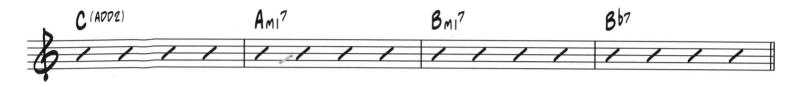

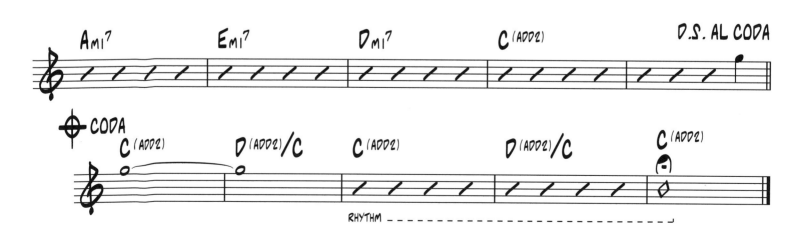

CD

COOL
FROM WEST SIDE STORY®

LYRICS BY STEPHEN SONDHEIM
MUSIC BY LEONARD BERNSTEIN ®

Eb VERSION

I FEEL PRETTY
FROM WEST SIDE STORY®

LYRICS BY STEPHEN SONDHEIM
MUSIC BY LEONARD BERNSTEIN®

CD
3 : SPLIT TRACK/MELODY
4 : FULL STEREO TRACK

Eb VERSION

49

JET SONG
FROM WEST SIDE STORY®

LYRICS BY STEPHEN SONDHEIM
MUSIC BY LEONARD BERNSTEIN®

Eb VERSION

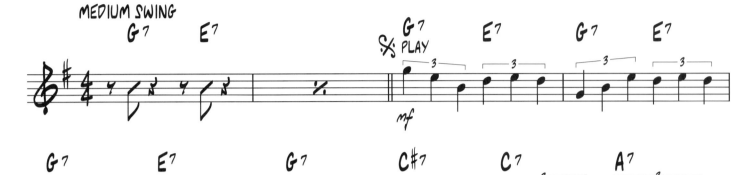

SOLOS (2 CHORUSES)

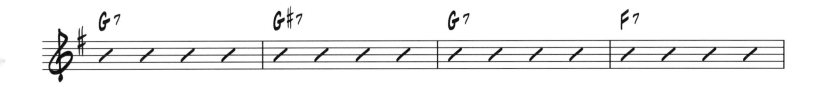

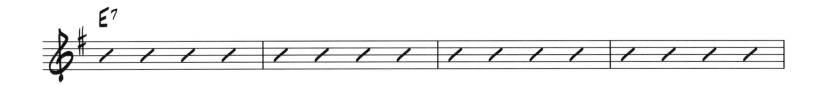

D.S. AL CODA

LUCKY TO BE ME

FROM ON THE TOWN

WORDS BY BETTY COMDEN AND ADOLPH GREEN
MUSIC BY LEONARD BERNSTEIN ®

Eb VERSION

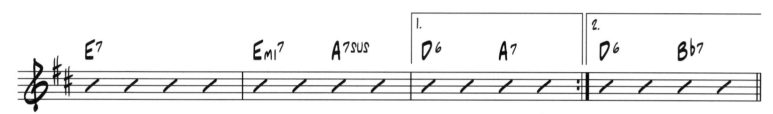

53

Mambo from the Dance at the Gym

FROM WEST SIDE STORY®

CD
◆ 9 : SPLIT TRACK/MELODY
◆ 10 : FULL STEREO TRACK

LYRICS BY STEPHEN SONDHEIM
MUSIC BY LEONARD BERNSTEIN®

Eb VERSION

CD

🎵 **11** : SPLIT TRACK/MELODY
🎵 **12** : FULL STEREO TRACK

MARIA
FROM WEST SIDE STORY ®

LYRICS BY STEPHEN SONDHEIM
MUSIC BY LEONARD BERNSTEIN ®

Eb VERSION

SOLO
A6   Ema7/G#   A6   Ema7

Bmi7   E7sus   Ama7   A6

E6/G#   F#mi7   C#mi7   F#mi7   C#mi7   G#mi7   /D#

D6   C#mi7   Emi7

B7sus   B/A   G7   Bmi7(b5)/E

A6   Bb6   A6   Bb6   D.S. AL CODA

⊕ CODA   Dma7   C6

Bb6   G7   Ama7

Some Other Time
FROM ON THE TOWN

WORDS BY BETTY COMDEN AND ADOLPH GREEN
MUSIC BY LEONARD BERNSTEIN ®

Eb VERSION

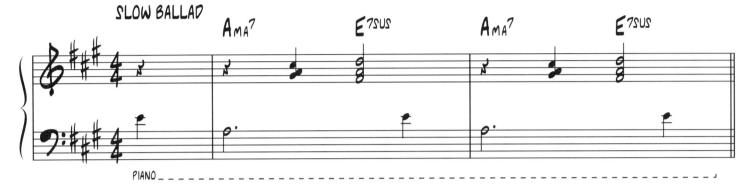

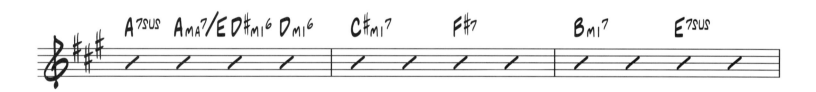

Somewhere
FROM WEST SIDE STORY ®

LYRICS BY STEPHEN SONDHEIM
MUSIC BY LEONARD BERNSTEIN ®

Eb VERSION

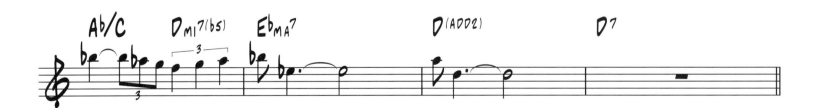

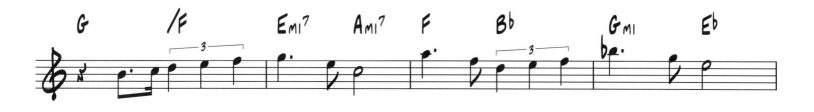

CD
19 : SPLIT TRACK/MELODY
20 : FULL STEREO TRACK

TONIGHT
FROM WEST SIDE STORY ®

LYRICS BY STEPHEN SONDHEIM
MUSIC BY LEONARD BERNSTEIN ®

Eb VERSION

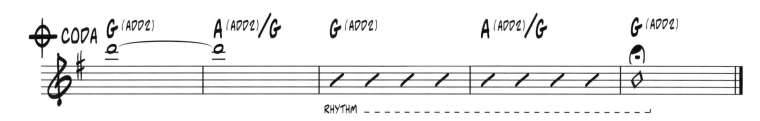

NEW YORK, NEW YORK

FROM ON THE TOWN ®

WORDS BY BETTY COMDEN AND ADOLPH GREEN
MUSIC BY LEONARD BERNSTEIN ®

Eb VERSION

65

NEW YORK, NEW YORK
FROM ON THE TOWN ®

WORDS BY BETTY COMDEN AND ADOLPH GREEN
MUSIC BY LEONARD BERNSTEIN ®

CD
13: SPLIT TRACK/MELODY
14: FULL STEREO TRACK

𝄢: C VERSION

PIANO

SOLO

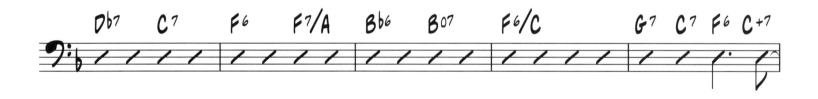

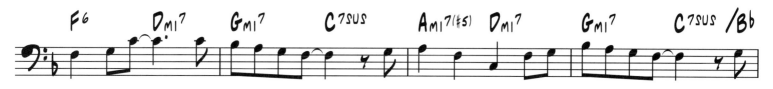

69

CD
1 : SPLIT TRACK/MELODY
2 : FULL STEREO TRACK

COOL
FROM WEST SIDE STORY®

LYRICS BY STEPHEN SONDHEIM
MUSIC BY LEONARD BERNSTEIN ®

♩: C VERSION
MEDIUM SWING

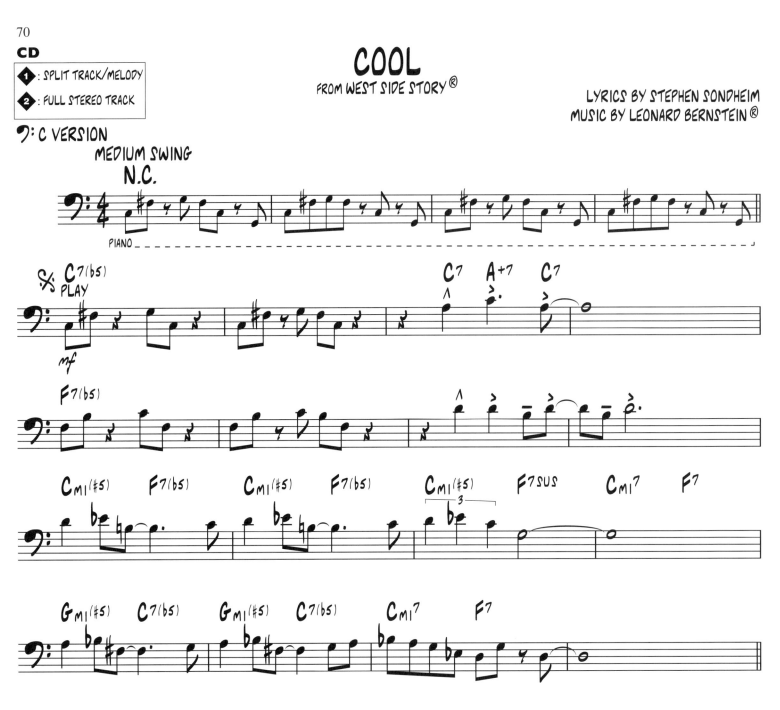

CD

3 : SPLIT TRACK/MELODY
4 : FULL STEREO TRACK

I Feel Pretty
FROM WEST SIDE STORY®

LYRICS BY STEPHEN SONDHEIM
MUSIC BY LEONARD BERNSTEIN®

𝄢: C VERSION

JET SONG
FROM WEST SIDE STORY ®

LYRICS BY STEPHEN SONDHEIM
MUSIC BY LEONARD BERNSTEIN ®

SOLOS (2 CHORUSES)

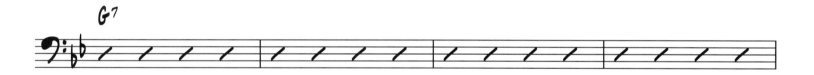

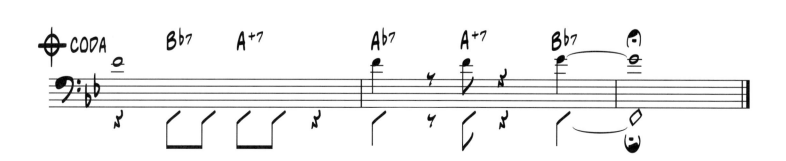

LUCKY TO BE ME
FROM ON THE TOWN

WORDS BY BETTY COMDEN AND ADOLPH GREEN
MUSIC BY LEONARD BERNSTEIN ®

CD
◆ 7 : SPLIT TRACK/MELODY
◆ 8 : FULL STEREO TRACK

𝄢: C VERSION

MEDIUM SWING

Mambo from the Dance at the Gym
FROM WEST SIDE STORY®

LYRICS BY STEPHEN SONDHEIM
MUSIC BY LEONARD BERNSTEIN®

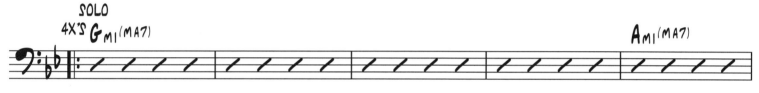

CD

11 : SPLIT TRACK/MELODY
12 : FULL STEREO TRACK

MARIA
FROM WEST SIDE STORY®

LYRICS BY STEPHEN SONDHEIM
MUSIC BY LEONARD BERNSTEIN®

🎼: C VERSION

SLOW LATIN

SOLO

C⁶ · · · | · · · · | Gᴍᴀ⁷/B · · | C⁶ · Gᴍᴀ⁷ ·

Dᴍɪ⁷ · Gᴍ⁷sus · | Cᴍᴀ⁷ · · · | C⁶ · · · | · · · ·

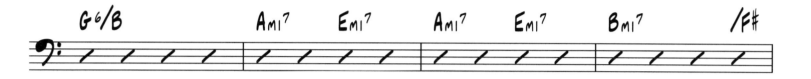

G⁶/B · · · | Aᴍɪ⁷ · Eᴍɪ⁷ · | Aᴍɪ⁷ · Eᴍɪ⁷ · | Bᴍɪ⁷ · /F♯ ·

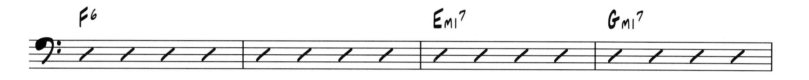

F⁶ · · · | · · · · | Eᴍɪ⁷ · · | Gᴍɪ⁷ · · ·

D⁷sus · · · | D/C · B♭⁷ · | · · · · | Dᴍɪ⁷(♭5)/G · · ·

C⁶ · · · | D♭⁶ · · · | C⁶ · · · | D♭⁶ · D.S. AL CODA

⊕ CODA
Fᴍᴀ⁷   E♭⁶

D♭⁶   B♭⁷   Cᴍᴀ⁷

SOME OTHER TIME

FROM ON THE TOWN

WORDS BY BETTY COMDEN AND ADOLPH GREEN
MUSIC BY LEONARD BERNSTEIN ®

𝄢 C VERSION

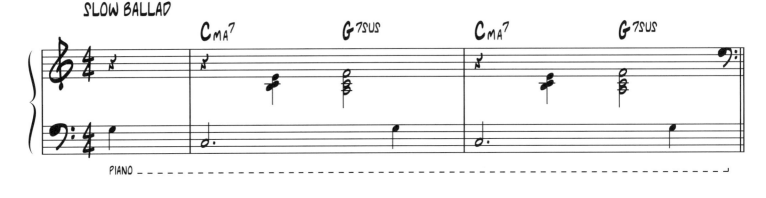

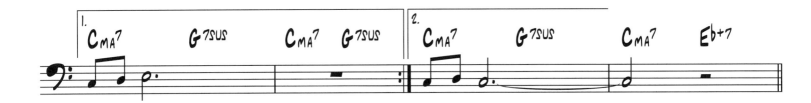

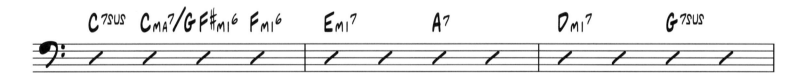

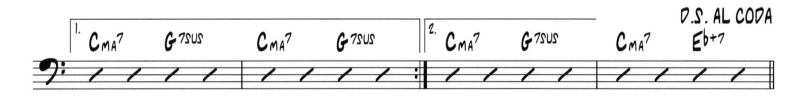

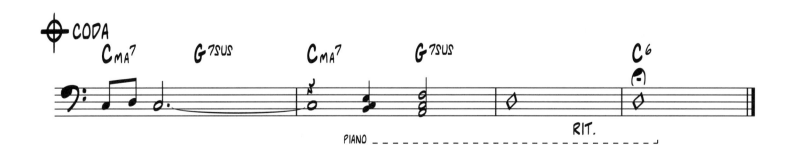

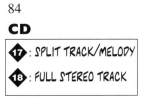

Somewhere
FROM WEST SIDE STORY®

LYRICS BY STEPHEN SONDHEIM
MUSIC BY LEONARD BERNSTEIN®

SLOW BALLAD

TONIGHT
FROM WEST SIDE STORY®

LYRICS BY STEPHEN SONDHEIM
MUSIC BY LEONARD BERNSTEIN®

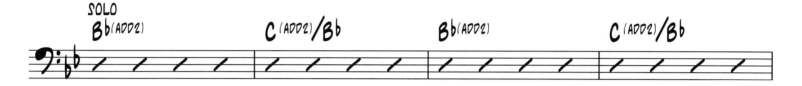

RHYTHM _